W9-CHN-917

Table of Contents

The Quilts

Introduction

How many times have you been browsing through the quilt shop and been enchanted by a big, beautiful print. You look at that fabric for the longest time, falling more and more in love with it, but then you walk away. You ask yourself, "How would I ever be able to use something with that large scale in a quilt?"

This pamphlet is the answer. There are lots of ways to use those big prints—and not just for borders or backs. Here you'll find ideas for cutting them up into small pieces, leaving them as big pieces and working them into many different, beautiful quilts.

Besides the large floral prints, Asian prints, paisleys and toiles, there's another whole category—novelty prints. These are plentiful in the marketplace. Some are whimsical, almost cartoonish. Others are thematic, cowboys or hot rods for instance. There are also lots of novelty prints perfect for children's quilts, like robots, paper dolls and fairy tale characters. These, too, can present a challenge for the quilter—until now. Turn the pages of this book and imagine your favorite giant poppy print or puppy dog fabric in one of these quilts. Hopefully you won't walk away from big prints next time one catches your fancy.

Working With Big Prints

Not all big prints are created equal. Designs may be directional or tossed, tightly packed or separated by lots of background. Each of these qualities needs to be considered when choosing a fabric and pattern. Each can present its own set of challenges, but none should be overlooked. Just be aware of the unique properties of each print and work with them rather than fight them.

When looking at the patterns, don't limit yourself to using fabrics that look "just like the photo." Fabrics come and go quickly in today's market and chances are you won't find the exact fabrics featured. You may want to find something similar, but keep an open mind when looking at patterns.

You may want to substitute a toile for a floral print. A quilt with a novelty print may be perfect for that Asian-inspired piece you've been saving.

Often when working with big prints you may need extra fabric so you can do some fussy cutting. Fussy cutting is nothing more than centering an element of the design in the patches or strips you are cutting. To some it may seem wasteful to fussy cut as you often have odd pieces of fabric left over—save them for another project. There's really no such thing as wasted fabric to the true quilter.

Novelty Prints

Novelty prints have been around for centuries and come in many scales. It wasn't uncommon to see small dogs or horseshoes on shirting prints from the late 1800s or toys and children in a small scale on prints from the 1920s and 30s. In recent years, however, novelty prints have exploded, both in the size of the prints and the number of offerings from which to choose. You can find novelty prints that reflect your favorite movie and cartoon characters, hobbies such as bull riding or fishing, trendy themes like fashion or tattoos, favorite foods and even pin-up guys and gals. These novelty prints make up into wonderful gift quilts that reflect the recipient's taste.

Opportunity Cloth

While not as plentiful as novelty prints, there are often opportunity fabrics available. These are sometimes referred to as "cheater cloth."

The designs may look like a patchwork or appliqué quilt but are printed on the fabric. They are usually meant to be used just as they are, without being cut. However, when you come across prints of this type, consider how they might look if cut up and used in another way.

Scattered Prints

Some big prints are scattered across the fabric with a lot of background showing. This is not a bad thing, but should be considered when choosing which quilts to make from them. Generally it is better to choose a quilt pattern that doesn't require cutting the big-print fabric into lots of small pieces. If there is strong contrast between the design and the background color, the edges of your piecing may become lost. Fussy cutting or using large pieces of a scattered design will result in a more successful quilt.

Packed Prints

Packed designs are just that—prints that have the pattern packed closely together without a lot of background showing. Even though they are large scale, prints of this type lend themselves well to cutting into smaller pieces and don't need to be fussy-cut.

Directional Prints

Directional prints can be handled two ways. You can ignore the directionality of the print and let pieces lie in every direction in the quilt. The results can be lovely. If you decide to do this, you'll want to take a few minutes when laying out the blocks to be sure that the design does, indeed, go in all directions. If 80% of the design is going in the same direction, the 20% that is different looks out of place. However, if the directional print is turned equally throughout the quilt, the pattern will look balanced.

You may prefer to keep the integrity of the design intact by making sure the direction of the print is the same throughout the quilt. Planning must start before cutting the fabric for the desired effect to be achieved. You will also want to be sure that you have enough fabric, especially if you are using it in the borders. Two of the borders will need to be cut lengthwise and two will need to be cut crosswise.

Scattered prints often have a lot of background showing.

Packed prints have the elements of the print packed closely together.

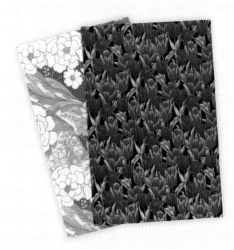

Directional prints may take extra planning before cutting.

General Instructions

Four Keys to Success

There are four basic things that you need to master to become a successful quilter:

1. Accurate cutting
2. A ¼" (6mm) seam allowance
3. Good pressing techniques
4. Measuring through the middle when adding your borders

Of course, you still need to quilt and bind your project, but if you pay attention to these four principles, your seams will match and your quilt top will lay flat.

Cutting

Accurate cutting is the first step in making quilts that go together easily and lay flat. Proper tools make cutting easy. Be sure that your rotary cutter has a sharp blade with no nicks, that you have a ruler that is at least 24" (61cm) long and that your mat is free of grooves.

The most common problem when cutting is letting the ruler wiggle as you make your cut. To avoid this, spread your fingers apart and place the fingertips on the half of the ruler that is closest to you. Do not lay your palm flat on the ruler. Place your rotary cutter next to the ruler and cut about half way across your fabric. Leaving your cutter in place, walk the fingers of the hand that is on the ruler up to the half of the ruler that is farthest from you. Press downward with your fingertips and continue making the cut.

Get familiar with your tools and learn to read your ruler correctly. If you are cutting many strips of the same size, it can be helpful to put a narrow piece of masking tape on the back of the ruler at the proper measurement. That way you can quickly see that you are lining up properly.

Did you know that your index finger should be placed on the top of your rotary cutter? Every brand of rotary cutter has a place for your index finger. If you grip your cutter by wrapping your fingers around the handle, your wrist is twisted and your hand is in an awkward position. By placing your index finger on the top of your cutter, you have a straight line from your elbow. This is ergonomically correct and won't lead to problems with your wrist or elbow.

Seam Allowance

Once you've cut your pieces accurately, it is important to sew them together using a ¼" (6mm) seam. Many sewing machines come with a ¼" (6mm) foot, or a special ¼" (6mm) foot can be purchased for them. If you do a lot of quilting, you may want to consider this. If you do not have a ¼" (6mm) foot, lay your acrylic ruler under your needle. Slowly, by hand, lower your needle until it just rests on the ¼" (6mm) mark. Use a piece of masking tape on your machine to mark along the edge of ruler. Use this tape as a guide when sewing your seams.

To make sure that you are using your ¼" (6mm) foot correctly, or that you have your masking tape in the correct position, do this experiment. Cut two 2" (5.1cm) strips of fabric, about 3" (7.6cm) long. Lay the strips together and sew along the long side with a ¼" (6mm) seam. Press. Now use your ruler to measure the width of the piece. It should be 3½" (8.9cm). If not, make adjustments and repeat the experiment.

Pressing

Pressing is just what is says—pressing. You want to press your fabrics and your seams without distorting them. It requires a gentle touch to do this. Whether or not to use steam is a matter of personal preference, but be aware that you are more likely to distort your fabrics if you are using steam.

When quilting, seams are generally pressed to one side as opposed to being pressed open. When pressing seams to one side, it is very important to press *from the front*. Lay the pieced patches on the ironing board. Since you will usually want to press your seam toward the darker fabric, lay the pieced patch with the darker fabric on the top. This will automatically make the seam allowance lay toward the darker fabric when you separate the patches. Before opening, give the seam a quick press to help marry the sewing threads to the fabric. Then gently lift the top layer of fabric. Use the side of the iron to lay it over and press. By pressing from the front in this manner, you will avoid leaving little folds or pleats at the seams. These little pleats can have an adverse effect when you join your blocks or rows together.

Borders

Borders on a quilt act like a frame on a picture—they serve to contain the action going on in the body of the work. Often this can be accomplished with a narrow border of an accent fabric and a wider border that matches the tone and value of the blocks. You can also use borders to increase the size of finished quilt. Each of the projects in the pamphlet gives you suggestions for choosing appropriate borders.

While borders may be the finishing touch to your masterpiece, if applied incorrectly, they can cause problems. If you merely cut a long strip and start sewing it to the edges of your quilt top, the border strip has a tendency to "grow," and the quilt won't lay flat. This occurs because the edges of your quilt include numerous seams which can become "unlocked" when you handle the quilt top. As you add the border to the edge of the top, each seam may open a little, causing the problem.

You can, however, create a quilt top that lays flat every time. It's as simple as measuring correctly and cutting the border strips the proper length before adding them.

After piecing and assembling the quilt blocks, find a flat surface on which to lay the finished top. Using a tape measure, measure the length of the quilt *through the middle*. Cut two strips of border fabric this length. Find the center of the strip and the center of the quilt top. This can be done by folding the fabric in half and finger pressing. Pin the border strip to the quilt top at the center point. Next, pin the top and bottom edge. Continue pinning every few inches, easing if necessary. Sew the seam with a ¼" (6cm) seam allowance. Press toward the border fabric.

Next, you will want to measure the width of the quilt top. Again, measure *through the middle*. This is what will ensure that your finished top will lay flat. Cut two strips of border fabric this length. Find the centers, pin, stitch and press. If there are multiple borders, repeat the steps, doing the lengthwise borders first.

Battings

There are many choices of batting to use in your quilt. Batting can be made from natural fibers like cotton, wool or even silk. They can also be made from polyester or a combination of a natural fiber and polyester. As well, there are different weights, thicknesses and lofts to consider. I mostly use cotton blends as I like the flat look and ease of care that they provide. Occasionally I use a polyester bat, but look for one that drapes well and doesn't have too much loft.

Layering and Basting

Once your quilt top is complete, you will need to make a quilt "sandwich" before you begin quilting. The quilt sandwich is made up of the quilt back, batting and the pieced top. The backing and batting should be at least 4" (10.2cm) larger than the quilt top.

1. After doing any necessary piecing of the backing fabric, tape the fabric, wrong side up, to a flat surface. Take care to ensure that the fabric is pulled taut.
2. Lay the batting over the backing and smooth out any wrinkles.
3. Lay the well-pressed quilt top, right side up, on top of the batting.
4. If you will be hand quilting, baste with long running stitches. If you will be machine quilting, baste with safety pins.

Prewashing Fabrics

To wash or not to wash—that is the question. If you buy good-quality cotton fabric, prewashing is not a necessity. There are several reasons not to prewash. First, unwashed fabric has a certain crispness. If you wash your fabrics, you remove the sizing. Secondly, there's not always time. Often when you get new fabrics, you just can't wait to cut into them! If you take the time to prewash, the inspiration may be gone. Lastly, when you wash a finished quilt, it puckers up just a bit around your quilting stitches, creating a desirable effect.

If you choose to prewash, don't just toss the fabric into the washer and dryer. You risk losing too much fabric due to frayed edges. Shrinkage is minimal with good-quality cotton fabrics. The main reason for prewashing is to remove any excess dye. You can do this easily without sending your fabrics for a spin in the washer and a tumble in the dryer. Follow these guidelines for prewashing:

1. Fill your sink or a basin with tepid water. Put your fabrics into the water and swish them around. If you notice a lot of dye being released, change the water and repeat until the water stays clear.
2. Place each fabric on a towel. Roll the towel around it and squeeze gently, then drape it on anything handy until it is nearly dry.
3. When the fabrics are still damp, press them with a dry iron until they are completely dry. If you wait too long, and the fabrics are completely dry, just spray them with a mist of water, wait a few minutes, then press.
4. You may want to use some spray sizing on your fabrics once you have pressed them dry. The sizing will give your fabrics body and make them easier to cut and stitch.

Quilting

There are so many choices for quilting today. Traditional hand quilting, quilting on your home sewing machine, midarm and longarm quilting machines, even computerized quilting machines.

While a longarm is good for large quilts, a regular sewing machine works well for smaller items like table runners and wall hangings. Many people prefer to take their finished quilt tops to a professional to be quilted.

All of the quilts in the pamphlet have suggestions for finishing. These are just suggestions and you should feel free to experiment and put your own finishing touch on your projects.

The fabric and pattern you've chosen have set the tone for your finished quilt. The quilting can enhance or detract from your finished project, so spend some time deciding how you're going to quilt it.

Thread color can make or break your quilting. When you have a pattern that has lots of contrast between the fabrics, consider using two different colors of thread for the quilting. I often quilt the dark areas of a quilt with dark thread, then go back and quilt the lighter areas with a matching light thread. Occasionally I'll leave small elements unquilted. This will allow those elements to stand out a bit.

Binding

1. Cut binding strips 2¼" (5.7cm) wide.
2. After cutting the required number of strips, piece them together with diagonal seams.
3. Press seams open.
4. Press the binding in half lengthwise, wrong sides together.
5. Trim excess batting and backing from the quilted top.
6. Beginning in the middle of the quilt, place the folded binding strip right sides together along the edge of the quilt. The raw edges of the binding and the raw edges of the quilt should be together. Pin one side.
7. Beginning 6" or 7" (15.2cm or 17.8cm) from the end of the binding strip, stitch with a ¼" (6mm) seam. Stop stitching ¼" (6mm) from the corner.
8. Backstitch.
9. Pivot the quilt. Fold the binding strip up at a 45-degree angle then back down.
10. Begin sewing at the top edge of the quilt.
11. Continue around all four corners. Stop stitching approximately 6" (15.2cm) from the

beginning of the strip. This will leave about 12" (30.5cm) of binding unsewn.

12. In the middle of this space, fold back the loose ends of the strips so they meet.

13. Mark a dot along the fold at this point.

14. Open the binding strips.

15. Pivot, aligning the dots, and sew the strips together with a diagonal seam.

16. Trim excess binding and attach the unsewn area to the quilt.

17. Fold the binding over the raw edge of the quilt so that it covers the machine stitching on the backside.

18. Stitch in place using a blind stitch. A miter will form at the corners of your quilt.

Gridded Triangle Method

Pre-printed papers are available with a grid drawn on them that allows you to make multiple half-square triangles at a time. This method is both quick and accurate. They are usually printed on newsprint and are easy to remove.

You can make your own triangle papers by drawing a grid onto paper. Newsprint works best, but copier paper also works well. To make two finished half-square triangles:

1. Cut a piece of lightweight paper 9" × 15" (22.9cm × 38.1cm). Draw 2⅞" (7.3cm) squares on the paper, three across and five down. Draw diagonal lines through all the squares.

2. Place the two fabrics for the half-square triangles right sides together. Pin the paper securely to the fabric. Stitch a ¼" (6mm) from both sides of the diagonal lines. Use a short stitch length to make paper removal easier.

3. Press. Cut apart on all the drawn lines, both straight and diagonal. Remove the paper and press the half-square triangles open. One paper will yield thirty half-square triangles!

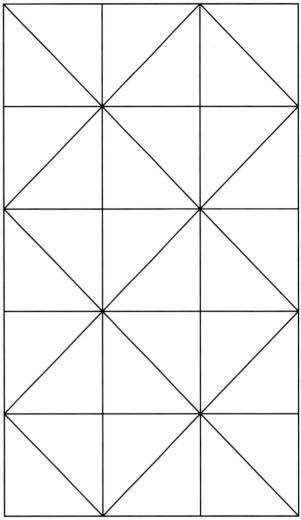

Triangle grid

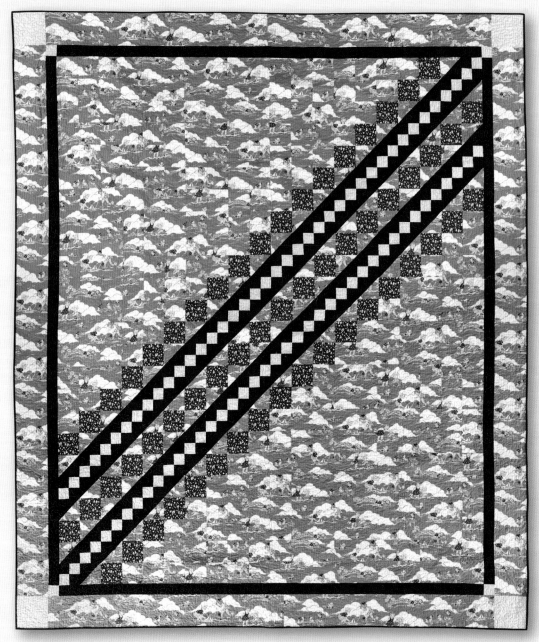

Pieced by Connie Nason and the author, quilted by the author

The Big Shake

You can really shake things up with this pattern. By cutting apart and rearranging the fabric an abstract feeling is created. The strong diagonal element breaks up the big-print fabric and adds a unique juxtaposition. Although this quilt is made from basic blocks—4" (10.2cm) squares, four-patches and half-square triangles—it gives the illusion of being much more difficult.

MEASUREMENTS

Quilt: 96" × 112" (2.4m × 2.8m)
Block: 4" (10.2cm)

FABRIC REQUIREMENTS

- 7½ yds (7m) big-print fabric for 4" (10.2cm) blocks and half-square triangles—more if fussy cutting
- 1 yd (92cm) red accent fabric for 4" (10.2cm) blocks
- 2¾ yds (2.5m) navy fabric for four-patches, half-square triangles and binding
- ⅝ yd (57cm) yellow fabric for four-patches
- 8½ yds (8m) backing fabric
- 100" × 116" (2.5m × 3m) batting

Choosing Fabric

This is a great way to showcase a novelty print like the one shown here. Look for a design with strong elements and good contrast, rather than one with a blended look. Whether you choose a floral or novelty fabric, the design elements can be quite large and you'll still have success with this quilt. When working with a multi-colored print, it's easy to draw upon the colors present for the accent fabrics. Small-scale prints, solids or fabrics that read as a solid work well for the accent blocks. *Consider making this quilt using the following types of fabric: scattered prints, directional prints or novelty prints.*

> **TIP**
>
> What are fabrics that "read as solid"? Fabrics that are tone-on-tone prints that don't have much variation in value. Every fabric company has its own version of a dimpled, tone-on-tone or subtle blender print available. Stepping back from these fabrics, the pattern shouldn't be obvious; it should look like a solid color.

CUTTING INSTRUCTIONS

Note: All strips are cut across the width of the fabric.

From the Big-Print Fabric, cut:

- **10**-6½" (16.5cm) strips for the border.

Note: If the print in your big-print fabric is directional, you will want to cut enough strips lengthwise for two of your borders.

- **38**-4½" (11.4cm) strips. Sub cut into **342**-4½" (11.4cm) squares.

> **TIP**
>
> You can shake the design up a bit more when sub cutting your strips into squares. Simply shift some of the strips to the right or left slightly so the pattern doesn't line up just the way it was printed when you sew the squares back together.

- **5**-4⅞" (12.4cm) strips. Sub cut into **39**-4⅞" (12.4cm) squares.

From the Red Fabric, cut:

- **7**-4½" (11.4cm) strips. Sub cut into **56**-4½" (11.4cm) squares.

From the Navy Fabric, cut:

- **5**-4⅞" (12.4cm) strips. Sub cut into **39**-4⅞" (12.4cm)squares.
- **5**-2½" (6.4cm) strips for four-patches.
- **9**-2½" (6.4cm) strips for the inner border.
- **10**-2¼" (5.7cm) strips for binding.

From the Yellow Fabric, cut:

- **5**-2½" (6.4cm) strips for four-patches.
- **1**-6½" (16.5cm) strip for border corners. Sub cut into **4**-6½" (16.5cm) squares, and **4**-2½" (6.4cm) squares.

Piecing the Blocks

Four-Patches

1. Join one 2½" (6.4cm) strip of navy fabric, right sides together, with one 2½" (6.4cm) strip of yellow fabric. Press toward the navy fabric. Repeat to make 5 strip sets. Press toward the navy.

2. Cut each strip set into 2½" (6.4cm) segments. Join 2 segments to make a four-patch as shown in Figure 1. Make 40 four-patches.

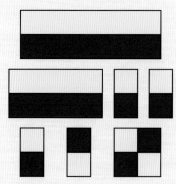
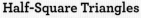

Fig. 1. Four-patches. Make 40.

Half-Square Triangles

1. Draw a diagonal line on the wrong side of 39 navy 4⅞" (12.4cm) squares. Place a navy fabric onto a 4⅞" (12.4cm) square of big-print fabric with right sides together. The diagonal line should go from the upper left corner to the lower right corner as shown in Figure 2.

Fig. 2.

2. Stitch a ¼" (6mm) on either side of the diagonal line and cut on the drawn line as shown in Figure 3.

Fig. 3.

3. Press to the dark fabric. Make 78 half-square triangles as shown in Figure 4.

Fig. 4.

Assembling the Top

1. Working on a design wall or on the floor, lay out the 4½" (11.4cm) squares, four-patches and half-square triangles as shown in the Assembly Diagram.

   Be sure the accent fabric in the four-patches creates a diagonal line.

Note: Work with the focus fabric. You may want to keep the design elements together or arrange them in a way that visually breaks up the original image.

2. Once you have the blocks laid out in a pleasing manner, join the blocks together in rows.

3. Press the block seams in each row in opposite directions. This will allow the seams in each row to nest with the seams in the row below it.

4. Join the rows together, working from the top down. Press.

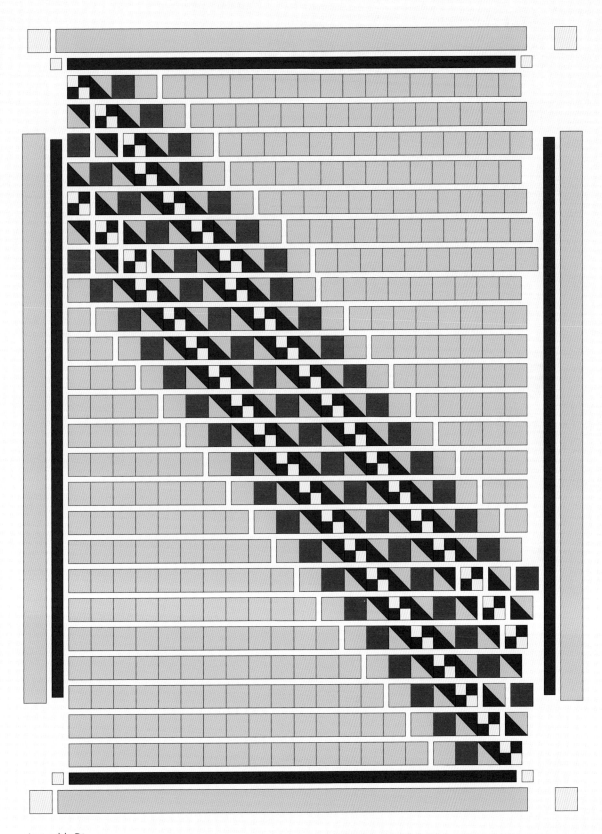

Assembly Diagram

Adding the Borders

Inner Border

1. Join the strips for the inner border together by sewing diagonal seams. Press open. Join all of the strips together until you have one long strip.

2. Measure the length of your quilt lengthwise *through the middle*. This will prevent you from having wavy borders. Mathematically this number would be 96½" (2.5m) but everyone's seam allowances vary, so be sure to measure.

3. Before adding borders to the side of the quilt, measure the top crosswise *through the middle*. This measurement should be 80½" (2m) but check your measurement to be sure. Cut 2 strips this length. Add a 2½" (6.4cm) square of yellow fabric to each end of these strips.

4. Attach borders from Step 2 to each side of the quilt. Press. Attach borders from Step 3 to the top and bottom of the quilt. Press.

Outer Border

1. Join the strips for the outer border together. Press seams open. Join all of the strips together until you have one long strip.

Note: If you cut the side borders from the length of the fabric, join them together and set aside before joining the top and bottom borders.

2. Measure the length of the quilt top lengthwise *through the middle*. This will prevent you from having wavy borders. Mathematically this number would be 100½" (2.6m), but everyone's seam allowances vary, so be sure to measure. Cut 2 strips this length.

3. Before adding borders to side of quilt, measure the top crosswise *through the middle*. This measurement should be 84½" (2.1m), but check your measurement to be sure. Cut 2 strips this length. Add a 6½" (16.5cm) square of yellow fabric to each end of these strips.

4. Attach borders from Step 2 to each side of the quilt. Press. Attach borders from Step 3 to the top and bottom of the quilt. Press.

Finishing Your Quilt

1. Cut your backing fabric into 3 equal pieces. Join together.

2. Prepare your quilt sandwich following the Layering and Basting instructions in General Instructions.

3. The options for quilting this quilt are wide open. You may want to quilt in the ditch vertically and horizontally. An allover design can be effective if it doesn't detract from the visual elements in the quilt.

4. Bind and label your quilt.

Pieced by Pat Hall and quilted by the author

The Great Gatsby

Here's a pattern that lets the beauty of the fabric, rather than intricate piecing, do all the work. Combining a fabric with strong graphics, like this Jazz Age design, with some coordinating prints in a trip-around-the-world pattern results in a stunning quilt. With nothing but straight-line sewing you can create a king-sized masterpiece in a very short time. To allow for the possibility of needing to fussy-cut the fabrics, this pattern is not strip pieced, but you'll find that the 6" (15.2cm) squares sew up quickly. There will even be nine squares left over that work perfectly for a pieced pillow!

14

MEASUREMENTS

Quilt: 106" × 118" (2.7m × 3m)
Block: 6" (15.2cm)

FABRIC REQUIREMENTS

- 5 yds (4.6m) black big-print fabric
- 2⅔ yds (2.5m) white accent fabric #1
- 2 yds (2m) blue accent fabric #2
- 2½ yds (2.3m) orange accent fabric #3
- 9¼ yd (8.5m) backing fabric
- 110" × 122" (2.8m × 3.1m) batting

Choosing Fabric

The simplicity of this design opens the door for creating a successful quilt from almost any style fabric. Large or small floral prints, geometric designs and even novelty prints can be showcased in this layout. The bold graphic fabric used as the big-print fabric in the sample was available in a white or black background. Both were incorporated into the quilt with a calmer blue and white to tone things down. To keep things from getting boring, a splash of orange livens it all up! *Consider making this quilt using the following types of fabric: packed prints, directional prints or novelty prints. You could also showcase embroidered blocks, appliqué blocks or photo transfers.*

CUTTING INSTRUCTIONS

Note: All strips are cut across the width of the fabric.

From the Big-Print Fabric, cut:

- **27**-6½" (16.5cm) strips. Set aside **12** strips for the border. Sub cut the **15** remaining strips into **90** 6½" (16.5cm) squares.

From the Accent Fabric #1, cut:

- **14**-6½" (16.5cm) strips. Sub cut into **84**- 6½" (16.5cm) squares.

From the Accent Fabric #2, cut:

- **10**-6½" (16.5cm) strips.Sub cut into **60**-6½" (16.5cm) squares.

From the Accent Fabric #3, cut:

- **5**-6½" (16.5cm) strips. Cross cut into **30**-6½" (16.5cm) squares.
- **10**-2½" (6.4cm) strips for inner border.
- **12**-2¼" (5.7cm) strips for binding.

TIP

While it's great to have multiple sizes of rulers at your fingertips, sometimes you don't have one that's wide enough for the strips you need to cut. If you have only a 6" (15.2cm) wide ruler, but need to cut 6½" (16.5cm) strips, try laying two rulers side by side to give you the width you require.

Piecing the Top

1. Work on a design wall or on the floor. Refer to the Assembly Diagram. Lay out the blocks to create a Trip-Around-The-World pattern.

Note: There will be nine blocks left over.

2. Once the blocks have been arranged, join them together in rows.

3. Press the seams in each row in opposite directions. This will allow the seams in each row to nest with the seams in the row below it.

4. Join the rows together, starting from the top of the quilt down. Press.

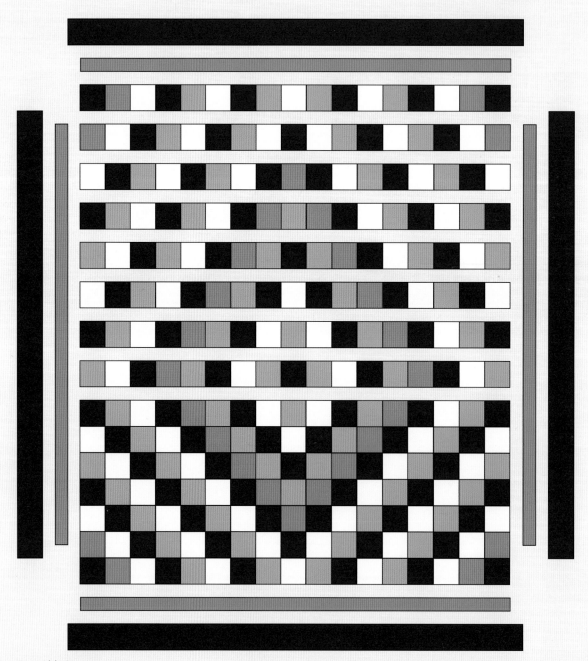

Assembly Diagram

Adding the Borders

1. Join the strips for the inner border together by sewing diagonal seams. Press open. Join all of the strips together until you have one long strip.

2. Measure the length of the quilt lengthwise *through the middle*. This will prevent you from having wavy borders. Mathematically this number would be 102½" (2.6m), but everyone's seam allowances vary, so be sure to measure.

3. Cut 2 strips the length of the quilt. Attach 1 to each side of the quilt. Press.

4. Now measure the quilt crosswise *through the middle*. This measurement should be approximately 94½" (2.4m), but check your measurement to be sure.

5. Cut 2 strips this length. Attach 1 to the top and 1 to the bottom of the quilt. Press. Repeat Steps 1–4 with the outer border fabric. Be sure to measure, and use your calculation in Step 2.

Finishing Your Quilt

1. Cut your backing fabric into 3 equal pieces. Remove selvages and join together.

2. Prepare your quilt sandwich following the Layering and Basting instructions in General Instructions.

3. Sometimes, as in the sample, the pattern in the fabric can dictate the quilting design. The great Art Deco lines of the fabrics called for an allover geometric design.

   This quilt would also be a good candidate for stitching in the ditch. Other options include diagonal quilting through each row of squares or an allover design.

4. Bind and label your quilt.

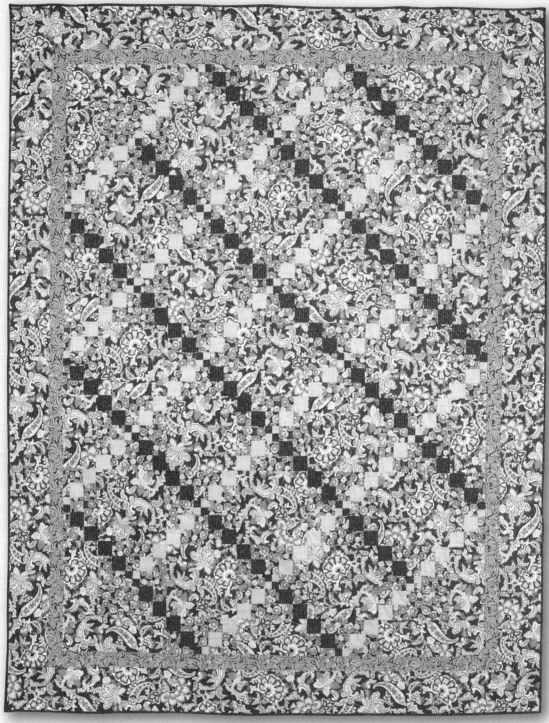

Big Bertha

This quilt is not only stunning to look at, it's very simple to piece. Strip sets eliminate piecing together lots of little squares. Bands of diagonal blocks create movement and interest on the surface of the quilt.

MEASUREMENTS

Quilt: 76" × 96" (1.9m × 2.4m)
Block: 10" (2.5cm)

FABRIC REQUIREMENTS

- 4¼ yds (3.9m) big-print fabric
- 2 yds (1.8m) medium scale floral
- 1½ yds (1.4m) red
- 1 yd (.9m) green
- ⅔ yd (61cm) print for inner border
- 5⅝ yds (5.1m) backing
- 80" × 100" (2m × 2.5m) batting

Choosing Fabric

If using floral prints, you need to find a large scale and medium-scale print that have the same colors throughout, or at least the same color in the background. This will insure that the blocks blend together and allow the diagonal squares to become the main design focus in the quilt. If you have a large-scale floral that you truly love, but can't find another to match it, you could repeat it in place of the medium-scale fabric. Depending on how strong you want the diagonal element to be, choose fabrics with little contrast or distinct contrast for the accent squares. Repeating the large-scale floral for the outer border is a good choice. *Consider making this quilt using the following type of fabric: packed prints. You could also showcase embroidered blocks, appliqué blocks, photo transfers or T-shirt blocks.*

CUTTING INSTRUCTIONS

Note: All strips are cut across the width of the fabric.

From the Big-Print Fabric, cut:

- **5**-10½" (26.7cm) strips. Sub cut into **17**-10½" (26.7cm) squares.
- **6**-5½" (14cm) strips. Sub cut into **10**-10½" × 5½" (26.7cm × 14cm) rectangles and **4**-15½" × 5½" (39.4cm × 14cm) rectangles.
- **9**-6½" (16.5cm) strips for the border.

From the Medium Floral, cut:

- **3**-1½" (3.8cm) strips.
- **3**-6½" (16.5cm) strips.
- **16**-2½" (6.4cm) strips.

From the Red Fabric, cut:

- **2**-1½" (3.8cm) strips.
- **11**-2½" (6.4cm) strips.
- **9**-2½" (6.4cm) strips for binding.

From the Green Fabric, cut:

- **2**-1½" (XXcm) strips.
- **11**-2½" (XXcm) strips.

From the Inner Border, cut:

- **8**-2½" (XXcm) strips.

Piecing the Strip Sets

Note: There are five different blocks that make up the body of the quilt. Strip piecing certain units will make assembling easier.

Strip Set A

1. Join a 1½" (3.8cm) red strip with a 1½" (3.8cm) green strip. Press toward the green. Repeat to make a second strip set.

2. Cut into forty-six 1½" (3.8cm) two-patch segments. Set 10 segments aside.

3. Join remaining segments to make 18 four-patch blocks.

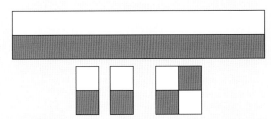

Fig. 1. Strip Set A. Two- and Four-Patches.

Strip Set B

1. Cut one 2½" (6.4cm) square from the end of six 2½" (6.4cm) green strips, six 2½" (6.4cm) red strips and nine 2½" (6.4cm) medium floral strips. Set aside. These will be used in Strip Set D and E.

2. Use the remaining strips from Step 1 to make 3 Strip Set B.

3. Cut into forty-two 2½" (6.4cm) segments.

Fig. 2. Strip Set B. Make 3. Cut into 42 segments.

Strip Set C

1. Join a red and green 2½" (6.4cm) strip to each side of a medium floral 6½" (16.5cm) strip to make Strip Set C. Make 3.

2. Cut into forty-two 2½" (6.4cm) segments.

Fig. 3. Strip Set C. Make 3. Cut into 42.

Strip Set D-Red and Strip Set D-Green

1. From a 2½" (6.4cm) medium floral strip, cut four 8½" (21.6cm) rectangles.

2. Join a red 2½" (6.4cm) square to one end of a rectangle. Strip Set D-Red. Make 2.

3. Join a green 2½" (XXcm) square to 1 end of a rectangle. Strip Set D-Green. Make 2.

Fig. 4. Strip Set D. Make 2 of each color.

Strip Set E-Red and Strip Set E-Green

1. From a 2½" (6.4cm) medium floral stip, cut four 6½" (16.5cm) rectangles.

2. Join a red 2½" (6.4cm) square and a floral 2½" (6.4cm) square to 1 end of a rectangle. Strip Set E-Red. Make 2.

3. Join a green 2½" (6.4cm) square and a floral 2½" (6.4cm) square to 1 end of a rectangle. Strip Set E-Green. Make 2.

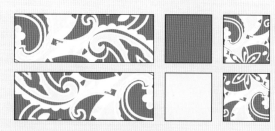

Fig. 5. Strip Set E. Make 2 of each color.

Strip Set F

1. From three 1½" (3.8cm) strips of medium floral, cut twenty 4½" (11.4cm) rectangles.

2. Add a rectangle to each side of a red/green two-patch. Make 10.

Fig. 6. Strip Set F. Make 10.

Strip Set G

1. From five 2½" (6.4cm) floral strips, cut thirty-six 4½" (11.4cm) rectangles.

2. Add a rectangle to each side of a four-patch. Check for orientation of the four-patch, being sure the red patch is in the upper left corner. Make 18.

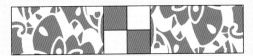

Fig. 7. Strip Set G. Make 18.

Piecing the Blocks

1. Join a Strip Set F to a Strip Set B and a Strip Set C. Note the orientation of the green squares as shown in Fig. 8. Press. Make 4.

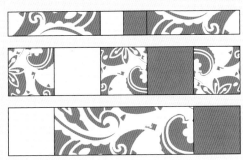

Fig. 8. Make 4.

2. Join a Strip Set F to a Strip Set B and a Strip Set C. Note the orientation of the red squares as shown in Fig. 9. Make 6.

Fig. 9. Make 6.

3. Join a Strip Set D-Green, Strip Set E-Green, Strip Set G, Strip Set B and Strip Set C. Note the orientation of the green squares a shown in Fig. 10. Press. Make 2.

Fig. 10. Make 2.

4. Join a Strip Set D-Red, Strip Set E-Red, Strip Set G, Strip Set B and Strip Set C. Note the orientation of the red squares, as shown in Fig. 11. Press. Make 2.

Fig. 11. Make 2.

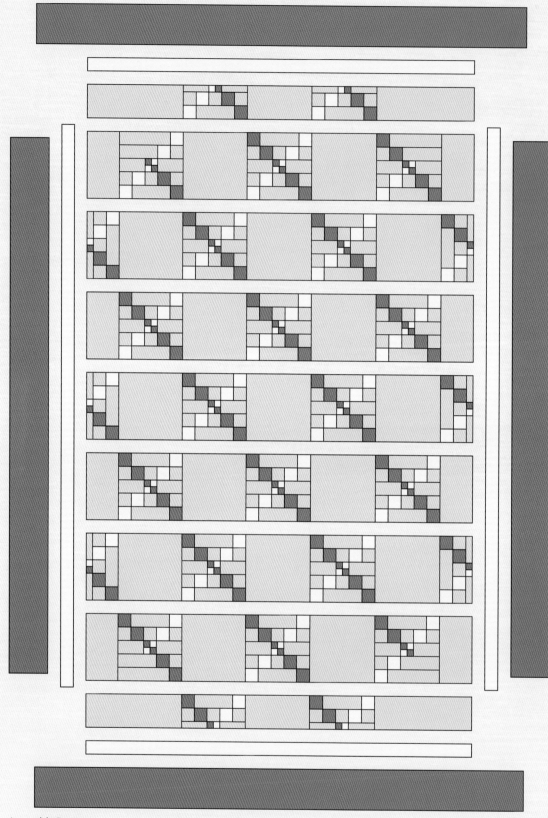

Assembly Diagram

5. Join a Strip Set C, Strip Set B, Strip Set G, Strip Set B and Strip Set C. Note orientation of red and green squares as shown in Fig. 12. Press. Make 14.

Fig. 12. Make 14.

Assembling the Top

1. Working on a design wall, or on the floor, lay out the blocks and big-print fabrics as shown in the Assembly Diagram. Check the orientation of the diagonal lines of color.

2. Join the blocks together in rows.

3. Press the seams toward the large floral blocks. This will allow the seams in each row to nest with the seams row below it.

4. Join the rows together, starting at the top of the quilt. Press.

Adding the Borders

1. Join the strips for the inner border together by sewing diagonal seams. Press. Join all of the strips together until you have 1 long strip.

2. Measure the length of the quilt lengthwise through the middle. This will prevent you from having wavy borders. Mathematically this number would be 80½" (2m), but everyone's seam allowances vary, so be sure to measure. Cut 2 strips the length of the quilt. Attach 1 to each side of the quilt. Press.

3. Now measure the quilt crosswise through the middle. This measurement should be approximately 64½" (1.6m), but check the measurement to be sure. Cut 2 strips this length. Add them to the top and bottom of your quilt. Press.

4. Repeat Steps 1–3 with your outer border fabric.

Finishing Your Quilt

1. Cut the backing fabric into 2 equal pieces. Remove selvages and join together.

2. Prepare your quilt sandwich following the Layering and Basting instructions in General Instructions.

3. Because of the scale and busyness of the fabric, this quilt was quilted with a rather large stipple. Any fancy stitching would be wasted on a quilt like this, as the stitches will disappear into the design of the fabric. However, the stipple did not go through the red and green squares, allowing them to stand out from the rest of the design.

4. Bind and label the quilt.

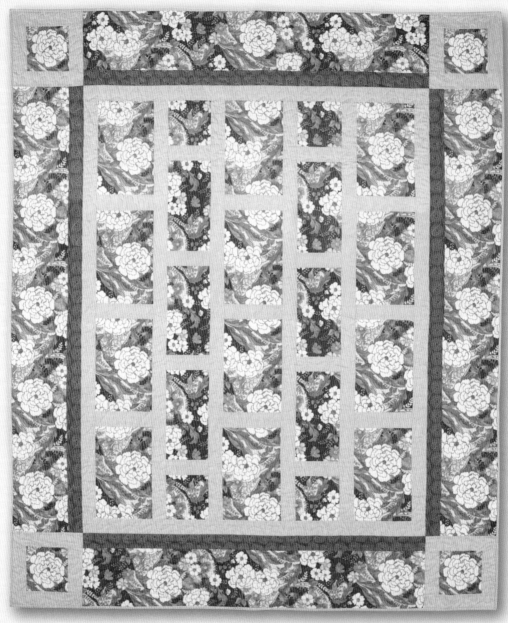

Pieced and quilted by the author

Grandeur

This quilt really shows off the beautiful floral fabric. The irregular placement of the sashings creates interest but doesn't detract from the design in the large-scale print. The subtle colors of the sashing and inner border also keep the design calm. This quilt also has a pieced back that incorporates strips left over from cutting the fabrics for the quilt top.

MEASUREMENTS

Quilt: 68" × 80" (1.7m × 2m)

FABRIC REQUIREMENTS

- 4½ yds (4.2m) big-print fabric
- 1⅝ yds (1.5m) green sashing fabric
- ½ yd (45.7cm) red inner border fabric
- ¾ yd (68.6cm) binding
- 72" × 84" (1.8m × 2.1m) batting
- 5 yds (4.6m) backing

Choosing Fabric

The large floral fabric used in this quilt was directional but a carefully thought out cutting plan keeps the elements flowing. While this is a splendid way to use a big, beautiful floral print, the sashing also reminds me of strips of film. Why not try incorporating photo transfers in this project? *Consider making this quilt using the following type of fabrics: scattered prints, directional prints or novelty prints. You could also showcase embroidered blocks, appliqué blocks, photo transfers or T-shirt blocks.*

CUTTING INSTRUCTIONS

From the Big-Print Fabric, cut:

Note: You may want to keep track of the layout of the big-print fabric and reassemble it in the same order that it was before cutting.

1. Cut a 54" (1.4cm) piece. Open it, press and trim away the selvages.

2. Turn the fabric lengthwise and cut **5** strips in this order: 8½" (21.6cm), 6½" (16.5cm), 8½" (21.6cm), 6½" (16.5cm), 8½" (21.6cm).

3. From the 8½" (21.6cm) strips cut **4**-8½" × 13" (21.6cm × 33cm) rectangles.

4. From the 6½" (16.5cm) strips cut, *in order*, **1**-6½" (16.5cm) square, **2**-6½" × 12½" (16.5cm × 31.8cm) rectangles, and **1**-6½" (16.5cm) square.

5. From the remaining big-print fabric, cut, selvage to selvage, **4** strips 8½" (21.6cm) for top and bottom border and corners. Set aside 3 strips for the border.

6. From the fourth strip, cut **4**-6½"(16.5cm) squares, fussy cutting if desired.

7. Turn the remaining fabric and cut **2**-8½" × 60½" (21.6cm × 1.5m) strips for side borders.

Note: The remaining big-print fabric could be used on the back of the quilt.

From the Green Fabric, cut:

- **22**-2½" (6.4cm) strips. Set aside **12** strips for piecing.

- From the remaining **10** strips cut **9**-2½" × 8½" (6.4cm × 21.6cm) rectangles, **16**-2½" × 6½" (6.4cm × 16.5cm) rectangles, and **8**-2½" × 10½" (6.4cm × 26.7cm) rectangles.

From the Red Fabric, cut:

- **6**-2½" (6.4cm) strips.

From the Binding, cut:

- **8**-2¼" (5.7cm) strips.

Piecing the Top

Center

1. Working on a design wall or the floor, lay out the center of the quilt.

2. Alternate rows of larger blocks and smaller blocks. See Assembly Diagram.

3. Add 8½" (21.6cm) and 6½" (16.5cm) (based on the width of each particular row) horizontal sashings between the blocks. Join together in rows. Press toward the blocks.

4. Join together twelve 2½" (6.4cm) sashing strips by sewing diagonal seams. Press seams open.

5. From this long strip cut six 2½" × 56½" (6.4cm × 1.4m) strips for vertical sashing and two 2½" × 48½" (6.4cm × 1.2m) for horizontal sashing. See Assembly Diagram.

6. Add the vertical sashing strips between the rows of the blocks and to the outside edges. Press.

7. Add the horizontal sashing strips to the top and bottom. Press.

Corners

1. Sew a 2½" × 6½" (6.4cm × 16.5cm) green strip to opposite sides of a 6½" (16.5cm) corner square. Press.

2. Sew a 2½" × 10½" (6.4cm × 26.7cm) green strip to the top and bottom of the square. Press.

3. Repeat to make 4 corners.

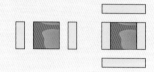

Border corner unit. Make 4.

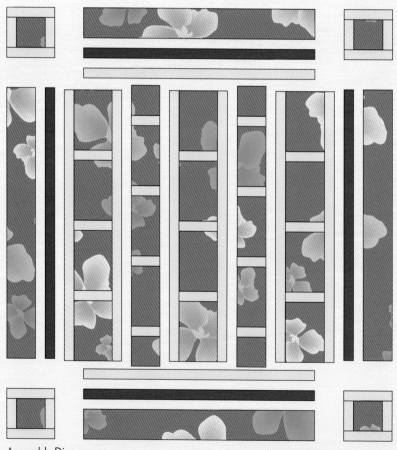

Assembly Diagram

Adding the Borders

1. Join the red strips for the pieced border together by sewing diagonal seams. Press open. Join all of the strips together until you have 1 long strip. From this long strip cut two 2½" × 52½" (6.4cm × 1.3m) strips and two 2½" × 60½" (6.4cm × 1.5m) strips.

2. Join the 3 strips of horizontal border fabric together, matching pattern as possible. Cut into two 8½" × 52½" (21.6cm × 1.3m) strips.

3. Trim vertical borders to 60½" (1.5m).

4. Join a red strip to 1 side of each of the border strips.

5. Sew the vertical border strips to the quilt top with the red strip to the inside.

6. Add a corner square to each end of the horizontal borders. Sew the horizontal border strips to the quilt top with the red strip to the inside.

Finishing Your Quilt

1. Cut your backing fabric into 2 equal pieces.* Remove selvages and join together. Prepare your quilt sandwich following the Layering and Basting instructions in General Instructions.

2. An allover design would work nicely on this quilt as long as the color of the thread doesn't detract from the fabrics.

3. Bind and label your quilt.

* Incorporate remaining big-print fabric if desired.

Grand Daddy

The famous photographer Edward S. Curtis, who documented the logging industry in the Northwest, said, "You aren't a logger until you have a one dollar pocket watch and your picture taken with a tree." Luckily, I have a few pictures of my grandfather taken in the woods, back in the days when it took two men and a very big saw to bring down the big trees. It was saws like those that undoubtedly inspired the name of this block.

MEASUREMENTS

Quilt: 77" × 91" (2m × 2.3m)
Block: 10" (25.4cm)

FABRIC REQUIREMENTS

- 5¼ yds (4.8m) big-print fabric for blocks and border
- 2¼ yds (2.1m) gold accent fabric
- 2½ yds (2.3m) black for side setting triangles, inner border and binding
- 5⅓ yds (4.9m) backing
- 81" × 95" (2.1m × 2.4m) batting

Choosing Fabric

To assure that the sawtooth element of this quilt is crisp there are two design elements to keep in mind. The accent fabric that is used for the half-square triangles should contrast sharply with the big-print fabric, and the colors in the big-print fabric should be similar in value or intensity. While scale isn't an issue, a packed design for the big-print fabric is preferable. The accent fabric should be a solid, or a fabric that reads as a solid.

With its 6" (15.2cm) center, the sawtooth can be used to showcase a special fabric. Here a tightly packed floral seemed just the thing to use to showcase all the sharp teeth created by the half-square triangles. If you choose to use this pattern for embroidered or appliqué blocks, match the saw tooth points to the background of the featured blocks. *Consider making this quilt using the following type of fabric: packed prints. You could also showcase embroidered blocks, appliqué blocks or photo transfers.*

CUTTING INSTRUCTIONS

Note: All strips are cut across the width of the fabric.
Note: For ease of construction, use the Gridded Triangle Method in General Instructions.

From the Big-print Fabric, cut:
- **4**-15" (38.1cm) strips for gridded triangles.Sub cut into **13** rectangles, 15" × 9" (38.1cm × 22.9cm).*
- **6**-6½" (16.5cm) strips. Sub cut into **32** -6½" (16.5cm) squares.
- **4**-2½" (6.4cm) strips. Sub cut into **64**-2½" (6.4cm) squares.
- **8**-8½" (21.6cm) strips for outer border.

From the Accent Fabric, cut:
- **4**-15" (38.1cm) strips for gridded triangles.Sub cut into **13** rectangles, 15" × 9" (38.1cm × 22.9cm).*
- **4**-2½" (6.4cm) strips. Sub cut into **64**-2½" (6.4cm) squares.

From the Inner Border, cut:
- **7**-2½" (6.4cm) strips.
- **3**-14¼" (36.2cm) strips. Sub cut into
- **5**-14¼" (36.2cm) squares. Cut each square in half twice diagonally to make **20** side-setting triangles. From the remainder of the strips cut **2**-8" (20.3cm) squares. Cut each square once diagonally for corner triangles.
- **9**-2¼" (5.7cm) strips for binding.

*If not using the Gridded Triangle Method, cut **15**-2⅞" (7.3cm) strips.
Sub cut into **192**-2⅞" (7.3cm)squares.

Piecing the Blocks

1. See General Instructions for instructions on Gridded Triangle Method. Make 384 half-square triangles. Press and trim dog ears from triangles.

Fig. 1. Half-square triangle. Make 384.

2. Join 3 half-square triangles with the big print to the right as shown in Figure 2. Make 64. Triangle-Strip A.

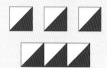

Fig. 2. Triangle-Strip A. Make 64.

3. Join 3 half-square triangles with the big print to the left as shown in Figure 3. Make 64. Triangle-Strip B.

Fig. 3. Triangle-Strip B. Make 64.

4. Add a 2½" (6.4cm) accent square and a 2½" (6.4cm) big-print square to either side of a Triangle-Strip B as shown in Figure 4. Be sure the accent square is on the left of Triangle-Strip B and the big-print square is on the right. Make 64.

Fig. 4. Add a 2¹/₂" (6.4cm) accent square and a 2¹/₂" (6.4cm) big-print square to either side of a Triangle-Strip B. Make 64.

5. Join a Triangle-Strip A to each side of a 6½" (16.5cm) big-print square as shown in Figure 5. Be sure the big-print triangle is toward the 6½" (16.5cm) big-print square. Press the seam allowances toward center.

Fig. 5. Add a Triangle-Strip A to each side of a 6¹/₂" (16.5cm) square.

6. Join a Triangle-Strip B (with the additional 2½" (6.4cm) squares) to each side of the block from Step 5. Be sure the big-print triangles are toward the 6½" (16.5cm) big-print square and that the 2½" (6.4cm) big-print squares are in opposite corners. Press the seam allowances toward center. Make 32 blocks.

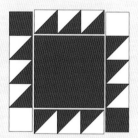

Fig. 6. Add a triangle-strip B to each side of a 6½" (16.5cm) square. Make 32 blocks.

TIP

Dog ears are the little points of fabric that extend beyond the seams when making half-square triangles. Trimming them makes a neater block and allows for easier matching of seams. A quick and easy way to trim dog ears is to place the pieced half-square triangle on a cutting mat before pressing it open. With the dog ears to the right and top, position a square ruler to the right top edge and cut off the ears. The square is trimmed and the waste stays on the mat for easy cleanup.

Assembling the Top

1. Working on a design wall or on the floor, lay out the Sawtooth blocks and setting triangles as shown in the Assembly Diagram.

2. Join blocks together in diagonal rows.

3. Press the seams in each row in opposite directions. This will allow the seams in each row to nest with the seams in the row below it.

4. Join the rows together. Press.

Assembly Diagram

Adding the Borders

1. Join the strips for the inner border together by sewing diagonal seams. Press open. Join all of the strips together until you have one long strip.

2. Measure the length of the quilt lengthwise *through the middle*. This will prevent you from having wavy borders. Mathematically this number would be 57½" (1.5m), but everyone's seam allowances vary, so be sure to measure. Cut 2 strips the length of the quilt. Attach 1 to each side of the quilt. Press.

3. Now measure the quilt crosswise *through the middle*. This measurement should be approximately 75½" (1.9m), but check your measurement to be sure. Cut two strips this length. Attach one to the top and one to the bottom of your quilt. Press.

4. Repeat Steps 1–3 with your outer border fabric. Be sure to measure.

Finishing Your Quilt

1. Cut the backing fabric into 2 equal pieces. Remove selvages and join together.

2. Prepare your quilt sandwich following the Layering and Basting instructions in General Instructions.

3. Depending on how busy the print is in your big-print fabric, the large center squares and wide borders on this quilt could lend themselves to some special quilting. However, if the print you chose is very busy, the work you put into the quilting may not be apparent. In such cases I often choose to do an allover design like a stipple or pantograph. Because of the strong contrast between the big-print fabric and the gold background, I chose not to do any quilting in the gold and quilted the rest of the quilt with a stipple in black thread.

4. Bind and label your quilt